Rookie
Read-About®
Health

I Have a
Cavity

by Lisa M. Herrington

Content Consultant
Jeffrey Pivor, D.D.S.

Reading Consultant
Jeanne M. Clidas, Ph.D.
Reading Specialist

Children's Press®
An Imprint of Scholastic Inc.
New York Toronto London Auckland Sydney
Mexico City New Delhi Hong Kong
Danbury, Connecticut

Library of Congress Cataloging-in-Publication Data
Herrington, Lisa M.
 I have a cavity/by Lisa M. Herrington.
     pages cm. — (Rookie read-about health)
Summary: "Introduces the reader to what a cavity is, how to prevent them, and
what happens when you get one"— Provided by publisher
Audience: Ages 3-6
Includes bibliographical references and index.
  ISBN 978-0-531-21038-3 (library binding: alk. paper) — ISBN 978-0-531-21111-3
(pbk.: alk. paper)
1. Dental caries—Juvenile literature. 2. Dental caries—Prevention—Juvenile literature.
3. Teeth—Care and hygiene—Juvenile literature. I. Title. II. Series: Rookie read-
about health.

RK331.H47 2015
617.67—dc23   2014035904

Produced by Spooky Cheetah Press
Design by Keith Plechaty

© 2015 by Scholastic Inc.

All rights reserved. Published in 2015 by Children's Press, an imprint of Scholastic Inc.

Printed in China 62

SCHOLASTIC, CHILDREN'S PRESS, ROOKIE READ-ABOUT®, and associated logos
are trademarks and/or registered trademarks of Scholastic Inc.

1 2 3 4 5 6 7 8 9 10 R 24 23 22 21 20 19 18 17 16 15

Photographs ©: Alamy Images/ableimages: 24; AP Images/Luca Bondioli: 30;
Dreamstime/Adauto De Araujo: 20; iStockphoto: 19 (dejanristovski), 23 top
(LICreate), 3 top left (rimglow), 23 bottom (robynmac); Media Bakery: cover
(Andersen Ross), 4 (Karin Dreyer), 27 (Moxie Productions), 31 (Richard Bartram),
7 (Shannon Fagan); PhotoEdit: 15 (Michael Newman), 15 inset (Spencer Grant);
Science Source/Biophoto Associates: 11 inset; Thinkstock: 19 inset (Elena Gaak),
3 bottom (HitToon), 16 left, 16 center (Trevor Buchanan), 16 right (vetkit), 28
(yellowpaul), 3 top right (Zheka-Boss), 11 (Александр Ермолаев).

Illustrations by Jeffrey Chandler/Art Gecko Studios!

Table of Contents

What Is a Cavity?

Open wide! It is time for a visit to the **dentist**. You have a **cavity**. Don't worry. The dentist will fix it!

A cavity is a broken-down part of a tooth. It starts as a hole. The cavity will grow bigger if it is not treated.

A dentist uses a mirror and other tools to look for cavities.

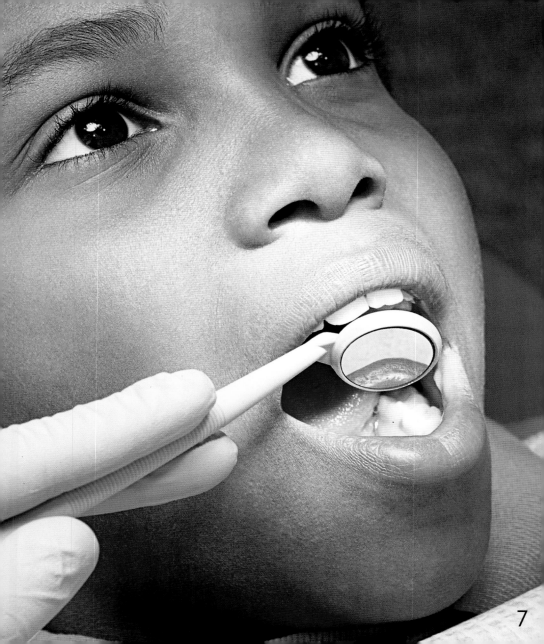

Types of Teeth

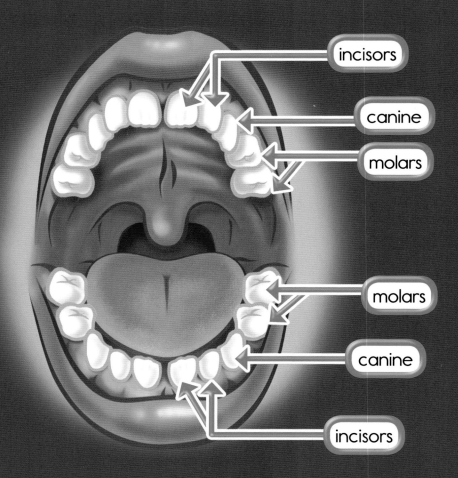

incisors

canine

molars

molars

canine

incisors

You need healthy teeth so that you can eat. So you need to protect your teeth from cavities.

Your teeth have different jobs to do. Incisors cut food. Pointy canines tear it. Molars crush and grind food.

What Causes a Cavity?

Tiny germs live inside your mouth. They form a sticky film called **plaque** (PLAK) on your teeth. When you eat or drink foods with sugar, the plaque makes acid. The acid eats away at your teeth. It causes cavities.

plaque

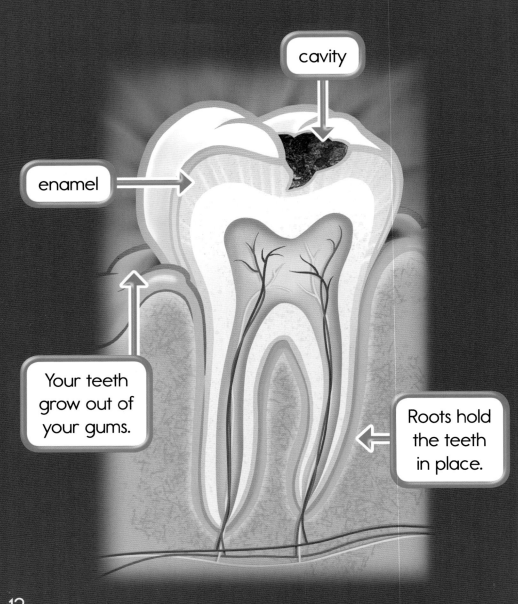

cavity

enamel

Your teeth grow out of your gums.

Roots hold the teeth in place.

Enamel is the hard outer layer of your tooth. A cavity can break through enamel. It can reach inside your tooth.

FAST FACT!

Enamel is the hardest part of your body.

Fixing a Cavity

Your dentist will look for cavities
when you go for a checkup.
Some cavities are hard to spot.
They can hide between your teeth.
The dentist may take an **X-ray**.

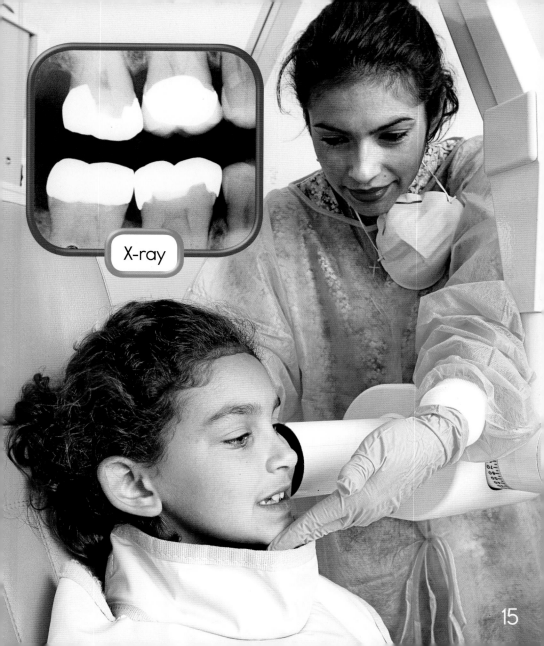

X-ray

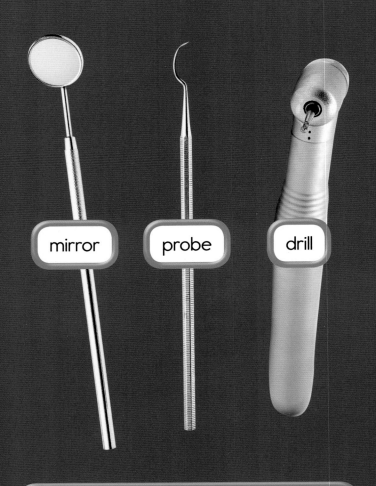

mirror

probe

drill

The dentist uses a mirror to look at your teeth. A probe is used to test if there are any soft spots in your teeth. The dentist uses a drill to remove your cavity.

Before starting on your cavity, the dentist will show you the special tools that will be used. The dentist will remove the soft part of the tooth around the cavity. The hole will be filled with a hard material. You now have a filling.

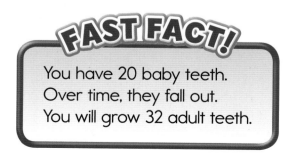

FAST FACT!

You have 20 baby teeth.
Over time, they fall out.
You will grow 32 adult teeth.

Go Away, Tooth Decay!

Taking care of your teeth can prevent cavities. Brushing helps get rid of plaque. Brush your teeth twice a day—in the morning and before bed. Use a pea-sized amount of toothpaste.

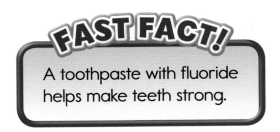

FAST FACT!

A toothpaste with fluoride helps make teeth strong.

Flossing helps keep your teeth clean. Dental floss is a special type of string. It removes food and plaque from between your teeth. You should floss once a day.

Eating right also keeps teeth healthy. Choose fruits and vegetables for snacks. Do not eat too many junk foods, like gummy bears and other candy. The sugar in these foods causes acid to form. That can lead to cavities.

Calcium helps build strong teeth and bones. It is found in some foods. Milk, cheese, and broccoli are good sources of calcium.

It is also important to visit the dentist twice a year. Healthy habits like these are the best way to keep from getting cavities.

Your Turn

Egg-cellent Experiment

Germs in your mouth make acid when you eat sugary foods. This experiment shows how acid can break down your teeth. (The egg is standing in for a tooth.) Before you begin, ask an adult for help.

1. Pour a cup of vinegar into a container.

2. Place an egg inside the container and close the lid.

3. Let the egg soak for two days. What happens to the egg?

Answer: The hard eggshell protects the egg the way enamel protects your teeth. Vinegar breaks down the eggshell. The acid in your mouth can attack enamel in the same way. Brushing and flossing keep teeth healthy and help prevent cavities.

Keep Cavities Away!

Here are some tips to prevent cavities. Which one is incorrect?

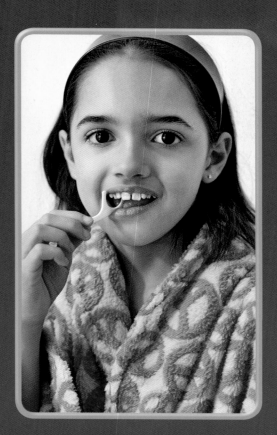

1. Brush twice a day.

2. Floss once a week.

3. Limit sugary snacks and drinks.

4. Visit your dentist twice a year.

Answer: 2. You should floss once a day.

Strange but True!

Having a cavity fixed is common today. Long ago, people had their cavities drilled, too. They did not have the tools and medicines we have today. So it was very painful! Some dentists made drills out of rock tips. Yikes!

Just for Fun

Q: What award did the dentist get?

A: A plaque!

Q: What did the cavity say to the dentist as she left the office?

A: Fill me in when you get back!

Glossary

cavity (KAV-uh-tee): hole in the tooth

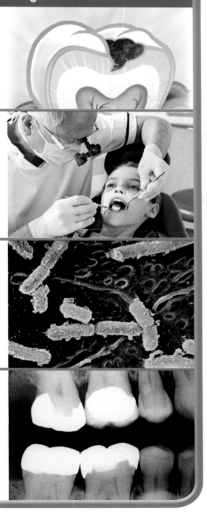

dentist (DEN-tist): person trained to clean and care for teeth

plaque (PLAK): sticky coating on teeth that can cause tooth decay

X-ray (EKS-ray): picture of the inside of a person's body

Index

Facts for Now

Visit this Scholastic Web site for more information on cavities:
www.factsfornow.scholastic.com
Enter the keyword **Cavities**

About the Author

Lisa M. Herrington is the author of many books and articles for kids. Lisa lives in Trumbull, Connecticut, with her husband, Ryan, and daughter, Caroline. She had a cavity filled while writing this book!